Everyday Agave

Recipes for healthy, everyday eating
using a low-glycemic sweetener!

Anne Astle

photography by Kari Astle

CREDITS
Layout and design: Robert Astle
Photography: Kari Astle
Food Styling: Johnyne Rees, Kari Astle, Anne Astle

Published by: Linwood Lodge Publishing
www.linwoodlodgepublishing.com
ISBN-13: 978-0-9790087-0-2
ISBN-10: 0-9790087-0-0

Printed by: Jostens, United States of America
First Printing, 2007

Table of Contents

Dedication

To Yahweh, our Creator, who opens His hand to satisfy the desire of every living creature (Psalm 145:16). The earth is full of Your wonders!

Acknowledgments

Thank you to my very supportive and talented family. Thank you to my husband, Rob, for lending his creative talents and sensitive palette to this project. Thank you to my sister-in-law, Kari, for volunteering her time and photography skills. Thank you to my mother-in-law, Johnyne, for her editing, and for being the pioneer of healthy cooking in our family and introducing me to agave. Thank you to my father-in-law, Tom, for his support and encouragement for this project.

Thank you to family and friends who tested recipe after recipe and gave me their expert opinions.

Introduction

Agave nectar is a low-glycemic sweetener derived from the agave plant, a desert succulent native to Mexico. Agave nectar is made from sap harvested from the heart of the agave plant. Traditionally used in making tequila, agave nectar is now gaining popularity as a healthier alternative to sugar because of agave's low-glycemic index, which is a measure of how fast the sweetener affects one's blood-glucose and insulin levels. Agave nectar is approximately 90% fructose, which absorbs slowly into the bloodstream.

Many varieties of agave are harvested to produce agave nectar. Blue agave has a higher fructose content compared to wild agaves, making its glycemic level lower. When purchasing agave nectar, be sure to inquire which type of agave plant was used in making that particular brand of agave nectar.

Agave can be purchased at health food stores in small quantities, but for those who plan to use it in "everyday" cooking, it tends to be prohibitively expensive if purchased this way. The most economical way to purchase agave is via the internet, where it can be purchased in bulk (for example, five-gallon buckets) – making the cost per ounce or cup more palatable.

Agave nectar looks similar to honey, but is looser in consistency. It comes in light, dark, and even an "extra dark" type that resembles molasses. Dark agave has a stronger flavor than light agave. Most of the recipes in this book call for light agave due to its more neutral flavor and color.

The following tips can be used to convert your favorite "sugar" recipes into "agave" recipes:

- Agave nectar is sweeter than sugar. When using agave to replace sugar, reduce measurements by 1/4 – thus, one cup of sugar is replaced by 3/4 cup of agave.
- Reduce oven temperatures by 25° F.
- Since agave is a liquid sweetener, reduce the amount of other liquids.
- Boiling agave will have a thickening effect, resulting in a range of consistencies from syrup to caramel to hard – depending on how long it boils.

For those who are calorie conscious, it is important to note that agave nectar is not a "low calorie" alternative to sugar. Agave nectar has 20 calories per teaspoon compared to sugar's 15 calories per teaspoon. Since agave nectar is sweeter than sugar by the same ratio, conversion to agave from sugar tends to have no effect on the total calories in a recipe.

The following chart will help you calculate how many calories are in recipes containing agave:

Agave Quantity	Calories
1 teaspoon	20
1 tablespoon	60
1/8 cup	120
1/4 cup	240
1/3 cup	320
1/2 cup	480
2/3 cup	640
3/4 cup	720
1 cup	960

Beverages

Mango Lemonade

6 1-cup servings

2/3 cup lemon juice	1 cup water
1/2 cup light agave	4 cups ice
1 cup mango (diced)	

1. Add ingredients to a blender in order listed.
2. Blend thoroughly.
3. Adjust amount of water and ice depending on desired consistency.

Non-Alcoholic Piña Colada
Yields 8 cups

3 cups fresh pineapple	3/4 cup light agave
1 14-ounce can coconut milk (unsweetened)	6-7 cups ice

1. Place all ingredients in a large blender. Make in 2 batches if using a small blender.
2. Blend until smooth. Serve immediately.

Perfect Party Punch

Yields 1 1/2 gallons

1 gallon water	2 1/2 cups light agave
1 46-ounce can pineapple juice	3 tablespoons citric acid (purchase at a pharmacy)
1 16-ounce can orange juice concentrate	

1. Mix all ingredients together.
2. Mix until orange juice concentrate has dissolved.
3. Pour into "freezer safe" containers. Place in freezer.
4. Thaw several hours before serving.

Frozen Café Mocha

2 servings

1 cup milk or unsweetened soy milk	1 tablespoon instant coffee
1/3 cup light agave	1 teaspoon vanilla extract
2 tablespoons cocoa powder	2 cups of ice

1. Add ingredients to a blender in order listed.
2. Blend on high until mixture is slushy.
3. Garnish with Whipped Cream (page 35) and Chocolate Syrup (page 23) if desired.

Fruit and Yogurt Drink

4 8-oz. servings

2 cups fruit (fresh or frozen)	1/2 cup light agave
1 cup plain yogurt	1 teaspoon vanilla extract
1 cup milk or unsweetened soy milk	

1. Combine all ingredients in a blender.
2. Blend until smooth. Chill before serving.

Strawberry Protein Shake
Yields 3 cups

1 cup low-fat cottage cheese	1/3 cup light agave
2 cups frozen strawberries	1/4 cup water

1. Add ingredients to a blender in order listed.
2. Blend until smooth. Add more water as needed.

Banana Split Smoothie
Yields 5 cups

16 ounces silken tofu	2 cups frozen strawberries
1 ripe banana	1 cup ice
1 cup pineapple	1/2 cup light agave

1. Add ingredients to a blender.
2. Blend until smooth.
3. Garnish with Chocolate Syrup (page 23) if desired.

Almond Milk

Yields 1/2 to 1 quart (depends on thoroughness of straining)

1 cup whole almonds	1/2 teaspoon vanilla extract
2 cups boiling water	1/2 teaspoon almond extract
1 cup water	1/4 cup light agave
1/2 teaspoon salt	

1. Place almonds in a medium bowl. Pour boiling water over almonds. Soak almonds for 8 to 10 hours.
2. When almonds are finished soaking, transfer to a blender along with soaking water.
3. Add additional cup of water and salt.
4. Blend on high for 2 minutes.
5. Using a fine mesh strainer, strain liquid over medium bowl. With a rubber spatula press almond milk through strainer. Discard almond paste or save for another use.
6. Repeat straining process until desired smoothness is acquired.
7. Transfer almond milk to a 1 quart container.
8. Add extracts and agave. Stir. Chill before serving.

Chocolate Milk

1 serving

1 cup milk or unsweetened soy milk	2 tablespoons chocolate syrup (page 23)

1.   Combine both ingredients. Stir thoroughly.

A beautiful agave specimen

Light agave nectar

Hot Chocolate

4 servings

1/4 cup cocoa powder	1/8 teaspoon salt
1/3 cup light agave	4 cups milk or unsweetened soy milk
1/2 cup water	1 teaspoon vanilla extract
3 tablespoons malted milk powder	

1. In a medium saucepan combine cocoa, agave, water, malted milk powder, and salt.
2. Bring to a boil over medium-high heat, stirring occasionally.
3. Add milk. Stir.
4. Heat to desired temperature.
5. Remove from heat. Stir in vanilla.

Sauces, Dressings, Toppings

French Dressing

Yields 4 cups

1 15-ounce can tomato sauce	1 teaspoon Worcestershire sauce
3/4 cup cider vinegar	1/2 teaspoon seasoned salt
3/4 cup vegetable oil	1/2 teaspoon onion powder
1/2 cup light agave	1/4 teaspoon black pepper
2 tablespoons salt	3/4 teaspoon xanthan gum (optional)

1. Combine all ingredients in a blender.
2. Blend until smooth.
3. Transfer to a covered storage container.
4. Store in refrigerator

Oriental Dressing
Yields 1 1/4 cup

1/2 cup vegetable oil	1 teaspoon sesame seeds
1/3 cup light agave	1/2 teaspoon ground mustard
1/4 cup pineapple juice	1/4 teaspoon ground ginger
2 tablespoons soy sauce	1/4 teaspoon dried minced garlic
2 tablespoons rice vinegar	1/4 teaspoon salt
1 tablespoon sesame oil	1/4 teaspoon xanthan gum (optional)

1. In a small bowl whisk together all ingredients.
2. Cover and chill.

Poppy Seed Dressing

Yields 2 1/2 cups

1 cup plain low fat yogurt	2 teaspoons lemon extract
2/3 cup vegetable oil	2 teaspoons poppy seeds
2/3 cup light agave	1 1/2 teaspoons xanthan gum (optional)
1/2 cup rice vinegar	

1. Place all ingredients in a blender.
2. Blend on low until all ingredients are combined.
3. Transfer to a covered storage container and refrigerate.

Sweet Balsamic Dressing

Yields 2 cups

1/2 cup light agave	1/2 cup olive oil
1 cup balsamic vinegar	1 tablespoon liquid lecithin (optional)

1. In a medium saucepan bring agave to a boil over medium heat. Boil for 5 minutes.
2. Remove from heat. Stir in remaining ingredients.
3. Allow to cool. Transfer to a covered storage container.
4. Does not need refrigeration.

Tomato Bacon Dressing

Yields 2 cups

1 cup mayonnaise	3 tablespoons apple cider vinegar
1/4 cup light agave	1/2 teaspoon salt
1/4 cup red onion (diced)	7 slices cooked bacon
1/4 cup tomato (diced)	

1. Combine all ingredients in a blender.
2. Blend until smooth.
3. Transfer to a covered storage container
4. Store in refrigerator

Ketchup

Yields 3 cups

1 12-ounce can tomato paste	1/2 teaspoon onion powder
1 cup light agave	1/4 teaspoon garlic powder
1 cup white vinegar	1/4 teaspoon ground mustard
2 teaspoons salt	

1. In a small saucepan combine all ingredients.
2. Bring to a boil over medium high heat. Reduce heat. Cover. Simmer for 15 minutes, stirring often.
3. Remove from heat and cool.
4. Transfer to a covered storage container.
5. Store in refrigerator.
6. For a smoother consistency, place cooled ketchup in a blender. Blend on high for 1 minute.

BBQ Sauce

Yields 2 cups

1 15-ounce can tomato sauce	2 tablespoons minced onion
2/3 cup light agave	2 teaspoons seasoned salt
1/2 cup apple cider vinegar	1/4 teaspoon hot sauce
3 tablespoons Worcestershire sauce	

1. Combine all ingredients in a medium saucepan.
2. Bring to a boil, then simmer uncovered for 30 minutes. Stir occasionally.
3. Remove from heat. Cool. Transfer to a covered container and refrigerate.

Chocolate Syrup
Yields 1 1/2 cups

1 cup light agave	1/3 cup water
1/2 cup cocoa powder	1 teaspoon vanilla extract

1. In a small saucepan combine agave and cocoa powder.
2. Stir over medium heat until cocoa powder is completely mixed with agave. Remove from heat.
3. Stir in water and vanilla until thoroughly combined.
4. Transfer to a container. Refrigerate.

Maple Syrup
4 servings

1 cup light agave	1/2 teaspoon imitation maple flavor

1. Combine agave and maple flavoring in a small saucepan.
2. Bring mixture to a boil over medium heat.
3. Boil for 5 minutes, stirring occasionally.
4. Remove from heat. Allow mixture to cool. Syrup will thicken as it cools.
5. Transfer to a storage container. Does not need refrigeration.

Berry Sauce

Yields 1 1/2 cups

1 cup berries (fresh or frozen)	2 tablespoons cornstarch
1/2 cup water	1/3 cup light agave

1. Combine all ingredients in a blender.
2. Blend until ingredients are combined and berries are partially crushed.
3. Transfer to a small saucepan.
4. Cook over medium heat until sauce thickens.
5. Transfer to a storage container. Serve slightly warm or chilled.

Blueberry-Cranberry Sauce

6 servings

3 cups fresh cranberries (washed)	1 teaspoon ground cinnamon
1 cup orange juice	1/4 teaspoon nutmeg
1 cup light agave	1/8 teaspoon allspice
1 cup fresh blueberries	

1. In a medium saucepan, bring cranberries, orange juice, and agave to a boil.
2. Reduce heat and simmer for 8 minutes. Stir occasionally.
3. Remove from heat. Stir in spices and blueberries.
4. Slightly mash blueberries with a spoon.
5. Allow mixture to cool. Transfer to a covered storage container.
6. Chill in refrigerator for 8 hours before serving.

Caramel Sauce

Yields 1 1/3 cups

1 cup light agave	2 tablespoons butter (melted)
1/4 cup heavy cream	2 teaspoons vanilla extract

1. Combine all ingredients in a medium saucepan.
2. Bring to a boil over medium heat. Boil for 5 minutes. Stir frequently.
3. Remove from heat. Transfer to a heat-safe container to cool. Store in refrigerator.
4. To serve, warm slightly in microwave.

Sweet and Sour Sauce

Yields1 1/4 cup

3/4 cup pineapple juice	2 teaspoons Worcestershire sauce
1/4 cup light agave	1/2 teaspoon sesame oil
1/4 cup apple cider vinegar	1/4 teaspoon garlic powder
1 tablespoon tomato paste	1/4 teaspoon ground mustard
1 tablespoon cornstarch	1/4 teaspoon ground ginger
1 tablespoon green pepper (finely diced)	

1. Whisk all ingredients together in a small saucepan.
2. Bring to a boil over medium heat.
3. Boil for 5 minutes.
4. Cool. Transfer to a covered container and refrigerate.

Frozen Café Mocha (page 5)

Cinnamon Raisin Bread (page 53)

Thai Peanut Sauce
Yields 1 1/3 cups

1/2 cup unsweetened peanut butter (smooth)	4 teaspoons ground ginger
1/3 cup light agave	2 teaspoons rice vinegar
1/4 cup unsweetened coconut milk	2 teaspoons chili powder
2 tablespoons sesame seed oil	2 cloves minced garlic
2 tablespoons lemon juice	1 teaspoon salt
1 tablespoon soy sauce	1/2 teaspoon ground coriander

1. Place all ingredients in a medium bowl. Whisk until smooth. (Ingredients can also be placed in a blender and blended until smooth.)
2. Cover and chill.
3. Warm slightly before using.
4. Use as a sauce over grilled chicken or tossed with noodles, or mix with vinegar and oil to make a great salad dressing.

Fudge Topping
Yields 1 1/4 cups

1 cup light agave	2 tablespoons butter
2 ounces unsweetened baking chocolate	1 teaspoon vanilla extract
2 tablespoons cocoa powder	

1. Combine agave and unsweetened baking chocolate in a medium saucepan.
2. Stir over medium heat until chocolate is melted and thoroughly combined with agave.
3. Add cocoa powder.
4. Turn heat to low. Stir continuously over low heat for 5 minutes.
5. Remove from heat. Add butter and vanilla. Stir until butter is completely melted.
6. Transfer to a heat-safe container to cool. Store in refrigerator.
7. To serve, warm slightly in microwave.

Cinnamon Butter
Yields 1 3/4 cup

1 cup butter (softened)	1 teaspoon cinnamon extract
1/3 cup light agave	1 teaspoon vanilla extract
2 tablespoons ground cinnamon	

1. Combine all ingredients in a medium bowl.
2. Beat with an electric mixer on high.
3. Place in container with lid. Store in refrigerator.

Meringue Topping

4 egg whites	1/2 teaspoon vanilla extract
1/2 teaspoon cream of tartar	1/4 cup light agave

1. In a small bowl, beat egg whites, cream of tartar, and vanilla with electric mixer on high for 1 minute.
2. Beat in agave 1 tablespoon at a time. Continue to beat on high for at least 4 minutes or until stiff peaks form.
3. Use according to selected pie recipe.

Whipped Cream

8 servings

---

1 cup heavy cream

2 tablespoons light agave

1/2 teaspoon vanilla extract

---

1. Beat all ingredients with an electric mixer on high for 4 to 5 minutes or until thickened.

Salads & Sides

Grilled Chicken Salad & Sweet Balsamic Dressing

4 servings (as a main dish)

8 cups green leaf lettuce (chopped)	1/2 cup silvered almonds (toasted)
12 slices cooked turkey bacon (crumbled)	4 grilled boneless chicken breasts (thinly sliced)
8 hard boiled eggs (diced)	Sweet Balsamic Dressing (page 19)

1. Arrange lettuce on dinner plates.
2. Top with bacon, eggs, and almonds.
3. Lay sliced chicken breast on top.
4. Pour dressing evenly over entire salad.

Mandarin Chicken Salad

4 servings (as a main dish)

12 cups Romaine lettuce (chopped)	1 cup rice noodles
2 1/2 cups cooked chicken breast (cubed)	1/2 cup sliced almonds (toasted)
2 11-ounce cans Mandarin oranges (drained)	Oriental Dressing (page 17)
1 8-ounce can water chestnuts (diced)	

1.   Arrange lettuce on dinner plates.
2.   Top with chicken, oranges, almonds, and rice noodles.
3.   Pour dressing evenly over entire salad.

Strawberry Spinach Salad

8 servings

5 cups fresh baby spinach	1 1/2 cups fresh strawberries (sliced)
1 cup shaved almonds (toasted)	1 1/2 cups poppy seed dressing (page 18)

1. In a medium sauté pan, lightly toast almonds over medium heat. Remove from heat once almonds are golden brown.
2. Place spinach on serving plates.
3. Top with almonds and strawberries.
4. Pour dressing on top.

Carrot Raisin Salad
6 servings

2 cups carrots (shredded)	1/3 cup light agave
3/4 cup raisins	1/3 cup sour cream
3/4 cup walnuts (chopped)	1/3 cup mayonnaise
1/2 cup red apple (diced)	1 tablespoon vinegar
1/4 cup celery (finely diced)	1 teaspoon vanilla extract
1/4 cup shredded coconut (unsweetened)	1/4 teaspoon ground cinnamon

1. In a medium bowl combine carrots, raisins, walnuts, apple, celery, and coconut. Set aside.
2. In a small bowl whisk together agave, sour cream, mayonnaise, vinegar, vanilla, and cinnamon.
3. Pour over carrot mixture. Stir to coat.
4. Chill before serving.

Cranberry Salad
28 servings

Step 1: Cherry Gelatine Base

1 envelope cherry-flavored unsweetened drink mix	2 cups water
3 packets unflavored gelatine	1 3/4 cups light agave

1. Combine above ingredients in a medium saucepan.
2. Warm over medium heat stirring until gelatine dissolves. Remove from heat.
3. Cool in refrigerator while processing fruit.

Step 2:

1-12 ounce package fresh cranberries	3 apples (quartered with seeds removed)
1 lemon (quartered with seeds removed)	4 bananas (diced)
2 oranges (quartered with seeds removed)	1 cup crushed pineapple (packed in fruit juice)

1. Using a food processor, grind cranberries, lemon, oranges, and apple.
2. Place ground fruit into large mixing bowl.
3. Stir in bananas, pineapple, and cooled gelatine mixture.
4. Cover bowl and place in refrigerator until mixture is firm enough to scoop with a spoon (at least 3 hours).

Sweet Cabbage Salad
16 servings

1 head cabbage	1 cup vinegar
1 cup onion (chopped)	3/4 cup light agave
1 cup carrot (finely shredded)	1 tablespoon dry mustard
1 cup celery (chopped)	1 tablespoon salt
1 cup olive oil	1 teaspoon celery seed

1. Chop head of cabbage using food processor.
2. In a large bowl, combine prepared vegetables. Set aside.
3. In a medium saucepan, combine oil, vinegar, agave, mustard, salt, and celery seed. Bring to a boil. Remove from heat.
4. Pour hot liquid over vegetables. Stir to coat.
5. Cover and chill at least 24 hours (flavor improves over time).
6. To serve, drain liquid.

Marinated Carrots

10-12 servings

2 pounds carrots	1/3 cup olive oil
1 green pepper (chopped)	1 tablespoon Worcestershire sauce
1 white onion (chopped)	1 teaspoon prepared mustard
1 cup tomato sauce	1 teaspoon salt
3/4 cup apple cider vinegar	
3/4 cup light agave	

1. Peel carrots. Slice thin.
2. Steam or boil until tender.
3. Combine carrots, green pepper, and onion in a medium bowl. Set aside.
4. In a separate bowl combine tomato sauce, vinegar, agave, oil, Worcestershire sauce, mustard, and salt.
5. Pour over prepared vegetables. Cover and chill.

Marinated Cucumbers

6 servings

3 large cucumbers	1/3 cup light agave
1/2 cup red onion (diced)	1 teaspoon celery seed
1/2 cup distilled white vinegar	1 teaspoon salt
1/2 cup water	

1. Peel cucumbers. Slice lengthwise. Scoop out seeds. Cut cucumbers into thin slices.
2. Place cucumbers and onion into medium bowl.
3. In a separate bowl, combine vinegar, water, agave, celery seed and salt.
4. Pour vinegar mixture over cucumbers and onions. Stir to coat.
5. Cover and chill at least 1 hour before serving.

Glazed Beets

7 servings

2 tablespoons apple cider vinegar	1/2 teaspoon ground cinnamon
2 tablespoons water	1/4 teaspoon ground cloves
2 teaspoons cornstarch	2 14.5-ounce cans sliced beets (unsweetened)
1/3 cup light agave	
1 tablespoon butter	

1. In a small saucepan combine vinegar, water, and cornstarch. Stir to dissolve. Add agave and butter. Bring to a boil over medium heat. Stir until mixture thickens.
2. Once mixture thickens stir in cinnamon and cloves. Add beets. Stir to coat.
3. Continue to cook until beets are desired temperature.

Creamed Corn

Yields 2 cups

4 cups frozen corn	1/2 cup light agave
1/2 cup cream	1 teaspoon salt

1. Thaw corn.
2. Transfer to a blender. Add remaining ingredients.
3. Blend on medium speed for 30 seconds.

BBQ Baked Beans

14 servings

2 cups BBQ Sauce (page 22)	1/2 cup red onion (diced)
4 15-ounce cans Great Northern Beans	

1. Preheat oven to 350°.
2. In a 3-quart casserole dish, combine BBQ sauce, beans, and onion.
3. Cover. Bake for 30 minutes.

Sweet Potato Casserole

6 servings

Filling:

3 1/2 cups cooked, mashed sweet potatoes	1/2 cup butter (melted)
1/3 cup light agave	1 teaspoon vanilla extract
2 eggs, beaten	1/2 teaspoon ground cinnamon

1. Preheat oven to 350°. Grease 8x11 casserole dish. Set aside.
2. In a medium bowl, combine mashed sweet potatoes, eggs, agave, butter, vanilla, and cinnamon. Stir. Pour into prepared dish. Spread evenly.
3. Prepare topping below.

Topping:

2/3 cup light agave	1/3 cup whole wheat flour
1 cup pecans (chopped)	1/4 teaspoon ground cinnamon

1. In a small bowl combine all ingredients.
2. Drop by spoonful evenly across surface of potatoes.
3. Spread lightly with spoon. Bake uncovered for 30-35 minutes.

Breads

Whole Wheat Bread

Yields 3 loaves

2 tablespoons active dry yeast	7 1/2 cups whole wheat flour
2 1/2 cups warm water	1/2 cup soy flour
1/3 cup light agave	1/4 cup ground flax seed (optional)
2 eggs	1 tablespoon wheat gluten
1/4 cup olive oil	1 tablespoon salt
1 tablespoon lemon juice	

1. Grease 3 medium loaf pans.
2. In a large bowl combine yeast and water. Once yeast has dissolved add agave, eggs, oil, and lemon juice. Stir.
3. In a separate bowl combine wheat flour, soy flour, flax seed, wheat gluten, and salt. Add to yeast mixture.
4. Knead dough by hand or with an electric mixer with dough hook. Dough should be slightly moist to the touch. If dough is too moist add additional flour 1 tablespoon at a time. Knead for 15 minutes or until dough is smooth and elastic.
5. Divide dough into three equal portions. Shape and place into prepared bread pans. Allow to rise until double in size. Allow to rise only once before baking at 350°. Bake for 30 minutes or until golden brown. Bread should sound hollow and feel firm when tapped.
6. Remove from pans to cool. For easy slicing, use an electric knife.

Cinnamon Raisin Bread

Yields 3 loaves

1 whole wheat bread recipe (page 52)	6 tablespoons light agave
2 cups raisins	Ground cinnamon

1. Grease 3 medium loaf pans with non-stick spray. Set aside.
2. Prepare whole wheat bread dough.
3. After dough has been kneaded, add raisins and allow dough to knead 1 additional minute.
4. Divide dough into 3 equal portions.
5. Roll out each portion of dough into 9x13 rectangles.
6. Spread 2 tablespoons of agave over surface of each rectangle.
7. Sprinkle generous amounts of cinnamon over surface of dough.
8. To form loaf start at narrow end of dough and roll towards opposite end. Once dough is rolled, pinch seams and ends. Tuck ends under and place seam down in medium loaf pan. Repeat.
9. Place loaves in a warm, draft-free area to rise. Allow bread to rise once before baking.
10. Bake at 350° for 25 minutes or until golden brown.

Blueberry-Banana Bread

Yields 2 large loaves

Oven 350°

3 cups whole wheat flour	2 teaspoons vanilla extract
1 cup oat flour	4 eggs
2 teaspoons baking soda	2 cups bananas (mashed)
1 teaspoon cinnamon	1 cup sour cream
1 teaspoon salt	2 cups blueberries (fresh or frozen)
1 1/2 cups butter (softened)	1 cup walnuts (chopped)
1 cup light agave	

1. Preheat oven to 350°. Grease 2-9x5 loaf pans. Set aside.
2. In a medium bowl sift together flours, baking soda, cinnamon, and salt. Set aside.
3. In a large bowl beat together butter and agave.
4. Beat in eggs, bananas, sour cream, and vanilla. Gradually stir in dry ingredients.
5. Fold in blueberries and walnuts.
6. Pour into loaf pans. Bake for 60 minutes. Insert knife into middle of bread to check for doneness.
7. Remove from oven. Cool in pans on a wire rack.
8. After bread has cooled, remove from pans and wrap with plastic wrap. Chill in refrigerator.

Pumpkin Bread

Yields 2 medium loaves

3 1/2 cups whole wheat flour	1 15-ounce can pumpkin (unsweetened)
2 teaspoons ground cinnamon	1 1/2 cups light agave
1 teaspoon ground ginger	3/4 cup vegetable oil
1/2 teaspoon ground cloves	3 eggs
1 teaspoon baking powder	1 teaspoon vanilla extract
1 teaspoon baking soda	Cinnamon Butter (page 33)
1 teaspoon salt	

1. Preheat oven to 350°. Grease 2 medium loaf pans. Set aside.
2. In a medium bowl combine dry ingredients. Set aside.
3. In a large bowl beat together pumpkin, agave, oil, eggs, and vanilla. Slowly mix in dry ingredients.
4. Pour batter into prepared pans.
5. Bake for 45-50 minutes or until knife comes out clean.
6. Allow bread to cool in pans before removing.
7. Slice and serve with Cinnamon Butter.

Cream Cheese Cinnamon Rolls

Yields 14 rolls   Oven 350°

1 tablespoon active dry yeast	2 teaspoons wheat gluten
1 1/4 cups warm water	1 teaspoon salt
1/4 cup light agave	1 tablespoon light agave
2 tablespoons olive oil	Ground cinnamon
1 egg	Cream Cheese Frosting (page 72)
4 cups whole wheat flour	1 cup pecans (chopped)

1. Grease 2-9" round cake pans. Set aside.
2. Combine yeast and water in a bowl. Once yeast is dissolved, add agave, oil, and egg. Stir to combine.
3. In a separate bowl combine flour, gluten, and salt. Stir into yeast mixture. Knead dough for 10 minutes until dough is smooth and elastic.
4. Roll dough into a 10" x 16" rectangle. Spread 1 tablespoon of agave over dough. Sprinkle with generous amounts of cinnamon.
5. Roll the dough lengthwise and seal edges. Slice dough into 14 portions using a piece of dental floss. Place 7 rolls in each cake pan. Allow to rise in a warm place until double in size.
6. Preheat oven to 350°. Bake for 20 minutes or until golden brown.
7. Allow cinnamon rolls to cool completely before frosting.
8. Sprinkle top with pecans.

Pecan-Caramel Rolls
Yields 14 rolls

Caramel-Pecan Sauce:

1 1/2 cup agave	1 tablespoon vanilla extract
1/4 cup heavy cream	1 1/2 cups pecans (coarsely chopped)
2 tablespoons butter	

1. Grease 2-9" round cake pans. Set aside.
2. In a medium saucepan combine agave, cream, and butter. Bring to a boil over medium heat. Boil for 5 minutes. Remove from heat. Stir in vanilla and pecans. Pour equal amounts of sauce into prepared pans. Set aside.
3. Prepare dough.

Dough:

1 tablespoon active dry yeast	4 cups whole wheat flour
1 1/4 cups warm water	2 teaspoons wheat gluten
1/4 cup light agave	1 teaspoon salt
2 tablespoons olive oil	1 tablespoon light agave
1 egg	Ground cinnamon

1. Combine yeast and water in a bowl. Once yeast is dissolved add agave, oil, and egg. Stir to combine.
2. In a separate bowl combine flour, gluten, and salt. Stir into yeast mixture. Knead dough for 10 minutes until dough is smooth and elastic.
3. On a lightly oiled surface, roll dough into a 10" x 16" rectangle. Spread 1 tablespoon of agave over dough. Sprinkle with cinnamon.
4. Roll the dough lengthwise and seal edges. Slice dough into 14 portions using a piece of dental floss. Place 7 rolls in each pan. Allow to rise in a warm place until double in size.
5. Preheat oven to 350°. Bake 20 minutes.
6. Place serving plates over pans and invert to remove.

Apple Raisin Muffins

Yields 12 muffins

1 3/4 cup whole wheat flour	1/2 cup milk
1 1/2 teaspoons baking powder	1/3 cup light agave
1/2 teaspoon baking soda	1/3 cup vegetable oil
1 teaspoon ground cinnamon	2 eggs (beaten)
1/8 teaspoon allspice	1 cup apples (chopped)
1/4 teaspoon salt	1/2 cup raisins

1. Preheat oven to 325°.
2. Grease muffin pan. Set aside.
3. In a medium bowl combine flour, baking powder, baking soda, cinnamon, allspice, and salt. Set aside.
4. In a separate bowl combine milk, agave, oil, and eggs. Add to dry ingredients. Stir.
5. Fold in apples and raisins.
6. Add approximately 1/4 cup of batter per muffin cup.
7. Bake for 15 minutes or until center of muffins are firm. Serve warm.

Blueberry Almond Muffins

Yields 12 muffins

Oven 325°

2 cups whole wheat flour	1/3 cup milk
1 1/2 teaspoons baking powder	1/3 cup vegetable oil
1/2 teaspoon baking soda	2 eggs (beaten)
1/4 teaspoon salt	2 teaspoons lemon extract
2/3 cup light agave	1 cup blueberries (fresh or frozen)

1. Preheat oven to 325°.
2. Grease muffin pan. Set aside.
3. In a medium bowl combine flour, baking powder, baking soda, and salt.
4. In a separate bowl, mix together agave, milk, oil, eggs, and lemon extract. Add to flour mixture. Stir to combine.
5. Fold in blueberries. (If using frozen blueberries, thaw and drain juice before adding to batter.)
6. Prepare topping.

Topping:

6 tablespoons butter	2 tablespoons light agave
1/2 cup whole wheat flour	1/4 cup sliced almonds
1/4 cup rolled oats	

1. In a small bowl combine flour and oats.
2. Add butter and agave. Cut butter into flour mixture until mixture becomes crumbly.
3. Toss almonds into mixture using a fork.
4. Add 2 tablespoons of topping to each muffin.
5. Press topping into batter lightly with a spoon.
6. Bake 18 minutes or until center of muffins are firm.

Cranberry-Orange Muffins

Yields 12 muffins   Oven 325°

2 cups whole wheat flour	1/3 cup vegetable oil
1 1/2 teaspoons baking powder	2 eggs (beaten)
1/2 teaspoon baking soda	1 tablespoon grated orange peel
1/4 teaspoon salt	1 teaspoon lemon extract.
2/3 cup light agave	1 cup cranberries (fresh or frozen)
1/2 cup orange juice	

1. Preheat oven to 325°.
2. Grease muffin pan. Set aside.
3. In a medium bowl combine flour, baking powder, baking soda, and salt.
4. In a separate bowl, combine agave, orange juice, oil, eggs, grated orange peel, and lemon extract. Stir into flour mixture.
5. Fold in cranberries. (If using frozen cranberries, thaw and drain juice before adding to batter.)
6. Fill muffin cups 2/3 full.
7. Bake 16-18 minutes or until center of muffins are firm.

Lemon Custard Poppy Seed Muffins

Yields 12 muffins

Filling:

1/3 cup water	3 tablespoons lemon juice
2 tablespoons cornstarch	1 egg yolk
1/3 cup light agave	1 tablespoon butter

1. In a small saucepan combine water and cornstarch.
2. Whisk in agave, lemon juice, and egg yolk
3. Whisk over medium heat until mixture thickens.
4. Remove from heat. Stir in butter until melted
5. Set aside while preparing muffin batter.

Batter:

1 3/4 cups unbleached white flour	1/4 cup lemon juice
1/4 cup poppy seeds	1/4 cup milk
1 1/2 teaspoons baking powder	1/3 cup light agave
1/2 teaspoon baking soda	1/2 cup vegetable oil
1/4 teaspoon salt	2 eggs (beaten)

1. Preheat oven to 325°.
2. Grease muffin pan. Set aside.
3. In a medium bowl, combine flour, poppy seeds, baking powder, baking soda, and salt.
4. In a separate bowl combine lemon juice, milk, agave, oil, and eggs. Stir into flour mixture.
5. Place 2 tablespoons of batter into each muffin cup.
6. Add 1 tablespoon lemon custard in center of batter.
7. Top each muffin with 1 tablespoon of batter. Spread batter to cover custard.
8. Bake 13-15 minutes or until center of muffins are firm. Serve warm.

Walnut Carob Chip Muffins

Yields 12 muffins

Oven 325°

1 3/4 cup whole wheat flour	1/3 cup vegetable oil
1 1/2 teaspoons baking powder	2 eggs (beaten)
1/2 teaspoon baking soda	1 teaspoon vanilla extract
1/4 teaspoon salt	3/4 cup unsweetened carob chips
3/4 cup milk	3/4 cup walnuts (chopped)

1. Preheat oven to 325°.
2. Grease muffin pan. Set aside.
3. In a medium bowl combine flour, baking powder, baking soda, and salt.
4. In a separate bowl combine milk, agave, oil, eggs, and vanilla. Add to dry ingredients.
5. Fold in carob chips and walnuts.
6. Add approximately 1/4 cup of batter per muffin cup.
7. Bake 15-17 minutes or until center of muffins are firm.
8. Serve warm.

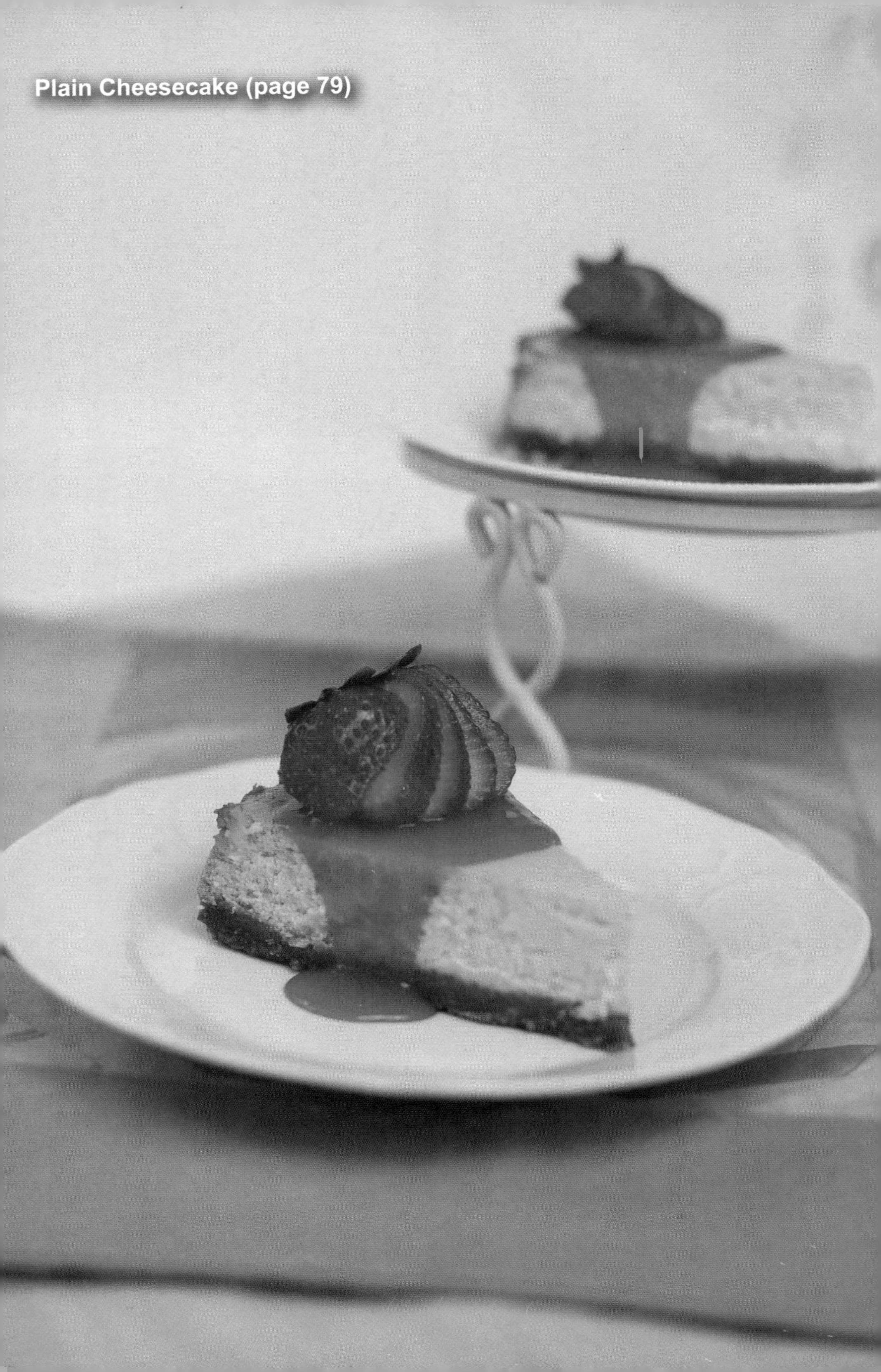

Plain Cheesecake (page 79)

Corn Bread Muffins

Yields 12 muffins

1 cup corn meal	3/4 cup frozen corn
1 cup whole wheat flour	1/3 cup light agave
1 tablespoon baking powder	1/2 cup cheddar cheese (shredded)
1 teaspoon salt	1/4 cup vegetable oil
3/4 cup milk	1 egg

1. Preheat oven to 325°. Grease muffin pan. Set aside.
2. In a medium bowl combine cornmeal, flour, baking powder, and salt. Set aside.
3. In a blender place milk, corn, and agave. Blend on low until corn is chopped into small bits. Add to flour mixture.
4. Stir in cheese, oil, and egg.
5. Add 1/4 cup of batter per muffin cup.
6. Bake 18-20 minutes. Serve warm.

Apple Pancakes

Yields 15 pancakes

1 cup whole wheat flour	2 tablespoons light agave
1 teaspoon baking powder	1 tablespoon olive oil
1/2 teaspoon baking soda	1 egg (beaten)
1/4 teaspoon salt	1 medium apple (peeled and diced)
1/4 teaspoon cinnamon	Maple Syrup (page 24)
3/4 cup water	
1/2 cup sour cream	

1. Combine flour, baking powder, baking soda, salt, and cinnamon.
2. In a separate bowl, whisk together water, sour cream, agave, oil, and egg. Stir into dry ingredients.
3. Fold in apples.
4. Heat and lightly grease frying pan.
5. Add two tablespoons per pancake to hot frying pan.
6. Brown pancakes on both sides.
7. Top with Maple Syrup.

Stuffed Baked French Toast

16 Servings

1 loaf cinnamon raisin bread (page 53) cut into 3/4" slices	2 teaspoons vanilla extract
8 eggs (beaten)	1/2 teaspoon ground cinnamon
1 1/2 cups milk	1-8 ounce package cream cheese (softened)
1 1/2 cups half and half	1/4 cup light agave

1. Butter a 9x13x2 glass baking dish.
2. Line bottom of baking dish with bread slices.
3. In a large bowl, combine eggs, milk, half and half, vanilla, and cinnamon. Pour 1/2 of mixture over bread slices.
4. In a small bowl beat together cream cheese and agave. Pour evenly over bread slices.
5. Place a second layer of bread on top of cream cheese. Pour remaining egg mixture on top. Cover. Refrigerate overnight.

In the morning:

3/4 cup light agave	1/2 teaspoon maple flavoring
1/2 cup butter (melted)	

1. Preheat oven to 350°.
2. Combine 1/2 cup melted butter, 3/4 cup light agave. Pour evenly over bread.
3. Bake uncovered 50 minutes.

Granola Cereal

Yields 9 cups

2 cups rolled oats	1/2 cup raisins
2 cups crispy brown rice cereal (fruit juice sweetened)	2 teaspoons ground cinnamon
1 cup puffed millet	1 cup light agave
1 cup almonds (chopped)	1/4 cup butter (melted)
1 cup almonds or peanuts (finely ground)	1 teaspoon vanilla extract
	4 egg whites (beaten)

1. Preheat oven to 170°. Lightly grease large, rimmed baking sheet.
2. In a large bowl combine dry ingredients.
3. In a separate bowl combine agave, butter, vanilla, and egg whites. Pour over dry ingredients. Stir to coat.
4. Pour mixture onto pan. Spread mixture and press down with a spoon or spatula.
5. Bake for 2 hours. Remove from oven. Use spatula or spoon to turn granola. Return to oven and bake a final time for 2 hours.
6. Remove from oven. Cool. Transfer to a covered storage container.

Desserts

Angel Food Cake
14 Servings   Oven 350°

2 cups egg white (approx. 18 eggs)	1 teaspoon almond extract
2 teaspoons cream of tartar	1 cup light agave
3/4 teaspoon salt	1 cup unbleached white flour
1 tablespoon vanilla extract	5 tablespoons cornstarch

1. Preheat oven to 350°.
2. Sift flour and cornstarch together. Set aside.
3. In a large bowl, beat egg whites, cream of tartar, salt, and vanilla and almond extracts on high with an electric mixer. Beat until soft peaks form. Gradually add agave and continue to beat until stiff peaks form.
4. Re-sift flour/cornstarch mixture over egg white mixture a small amount at a time, stirring by hand after each addition.
5. Pour into ungreased 10-inch tube pan. Place on lowest oven rack.
6. Bake 25-30 minutes. Remove from oven and invert cake over large plate until cake has completely cooled. Loosen cake before removing from pan.

Carrot Cake
12 servings

2 cups whole wheat flour	1 teaspoon vanilla extract
2 teaspoons baking soda	1 teaspoon almond extract
1/2 teaspoon salt	1 3/4 cup grated carrot
2 teaspoons ground cinnamon	1 8-ounce can crushed pineapple (drained)
3 eggs	
1 1/2 cups light agave	1/2 cup unsweetened coconut flakes
2/3 cup vegetable oil	1 cup pecans (chopped)
2/3 cup buttermilk	Cream Cheese Frosting (page 72)

1.   Preheat oven to 350°. Lightly grease and flour 2-9" round cake pans.
2.   Sift together flour, baking soda, salt, and cinnamon. Set aside.
3.   In a medium bowl, beat eggs, agave, oil, buttermilk and extracts with an electric mixer. Add to flour mixture. Beat on medium speed until blended.
4.   Fold in carrots, pineapple, coconut, and pecans. Pour into prepared pans.
5.   Bake for 20-25 minutes. Check center for doneness with knife.
6.   Place pans on wire rack to cool. Cool completely before removing from pan and frosting.

Cream Cheese Frosting

Yields 2 2/3 cups

2-8 ounce packages cream cheese (softened)	2 teaspoons vanilla extract
1/2 cup butter (softened)	1 teaspoon almond extract
2/3 cup light agave	

1. In a medium bowl beat cream cheese and butter with an electric mixer.
2. Gradually beat in agave, vanilla, and almond extracts until smooth.
3. Chill before using.

German Chocolate Cake

10 servings

4 ounces unsweetened baking chocolate	1 1/2 cups light agave
1/2 cup water	3/4 cup mayonnaise
2 cups whole wheat flour	4 eggs
1 1/2 teaspoons baking soda	2 teaspoons vanilla extract
1/2 teaspoon salt	Coconut-Pecan Frosting (page 74)
1 cup butter (softened)	

1. Preheat oven to 350°. Lightly grease 2-9" round cake pans. Set aside.
2. Place baking chocolate and water in a microwavable bowl. Microwave for 2 minutes, stirring after 1 minute. Chocolate should be thoroughly melted and combined with water. Set aside.
3. In a small bowl combine flour, baking soda, and salt.
4. In a large mixing bowl beat butter, mayonnaise, and melted chocolate with an electric mixer. Beat in agave, eggs, and vanilla. Gradually add flour mixture. Stir.
5. Pour into prepared cake pans. Bake for 20-25 minutes.
6. Cool on wire rack before removing from pans. Cool completely before frosting.

Coconut-Pecan Frosting

Yields 3 1/2 cups

1 cup evaporated milk	1 1/2 cups unsweetened coconut flakes
1/2 cup whipping cream	1 cup pecans (chopped)
1 1/4 cup light agave	2 teaspoons vanilla extract
1/4 cup butter	
4 egg yolks	

1. In a medium saucepan combine milk, cream, agave, and butter. Bring to a boil over medium heat. Stir occasionally. Continue to boil for 10 minutes, stirring frequently. Remove from heat.
2. In a small bowl beat egg yolks. Slowly beat in 1 cup of hot milk mixture into egg yolks. Return egg mixture to saucepan. Stir over medium heat until mixture comes to a boil and thickens slightly. Remove from heat.
3. Stir in coconut, pecans, and vanilla.
4. Transfer to a container to cool. Refrigerate. Return to room temperature before using.

Pineapple Upside-Down Cake

8 servings

1 1/4 cup light agave	1 cup whole wheat flour
1/4 cup butter (softened)	3/4 teaspoon baking soda
2 teaspoons vanilla extract (divided)	1/4 teaspoon salt
1 15-ounce can pineapple slices (packed in fruit juice)	1/2 cup mayonnaise
	1/3 cup vegetable oil
6 ounce jar maraschino cherries	2 eggs

1. Preheat oven to 325°. Lightly grease 9" cake pan. Set aside.
2. In a small saucepan bring 3/4 cup agave (reserving 1/2 cup for cake batter) and butter to a boil over medium heat. Boil for 5 minutes. Remove from heat. Stir in 1 teaspoon vanilla.
3. Drain pineapples. Cut pineapple slices in half. Arrange on bottom of pan. Place 1 cherry inside half circle of each pineapple slice. Pour agave over pineapple slices. Set aside.
4. In a medium bowl combine agave and mayonnaise with an electric mixer. Add oil, eggs, and vanilla. Beat until smooth. Set aside.
5. In a separate bowl combine flour, baking soda, and salt. Gradually mix into agave/mayonnaise mixture. Pour batter over pineapples.
6. Bake 30-35 minutes. To remove, invert cake over serving plate.

Whole Wheat Pound Cake

24 servings

1 cup butter (room temperature)	2 tablespoons lemon extract
1 1/2 cups light agave	1 teaspoon almond extract
4 eggs	3 cups whole wheat flour
3/4 cup sour cream	1/2 teaspoon baking soda
2 tablespoons vanilla extract	1/2 teaspoon salt

1. Preheat oven to 325°. Grease a 10" bundt pan with non-stick spray.
2. With an electric mixer cream butter and agave. Beat in eggs one at a time. Add sour cream, vanilla, lemon, and almond extracts. Mix until combined. Set aside.
3. In a separate bowl combine flour, baking soda, and salt. Add to wet ingredients. Stir until just mixed. Pour into prepared bundt pan.
4. Bake for 50 minutes or until knife comes out clean.
5. Cool in pan on wire rack 10 minutes before removing from pan. Serve at room temperature or chilled. Top with Berry Sauce (page 25) and Whipped Cream (page 35) if desired.

Chocolate Turtle Cheesecake

12 servings   Oven 300°

Crust:

2 cups sugar-free chocolate sandwich cookie crumbs	1/4 cup butter (melted

1. Preheat oven to 300°. Lightly butter sides of a 9" spring-form pan. Line bottom with parchment paper.
2. In a small bowl combine cookie crumbs and butter. Stir to coat. Press into bottom of spring-form pan. Set aside. Prepare filling.

Filling:

3-8 ounce packages cream cheese (softened)	3 ounces unsweetened baking chocolate (melted)
3/4 cup light agave	1 teaspoon vanilla extract
4 eggs	

1. Place cream cheese in a large mixing bowl. With an electric mixer, gradually beat agave into cream cheese. Next, beat in eggs one at a time until smooth. Add melted chocolate and vanilla. Stir until color of batter is uniform.
2. Pour batter over crust. Bake 45 minutes or until center of cheesecake is firm. Remove from oven. Turn oven off. Loosen sides of cheesecake with a knife. Place cheesecake back in oven. Leave in oven until pan is warm to the touch. Cover and chill.
3. While cheesecake chills, prepare Caramel Sauce (page 27).

Topping:

Caramel Sauce (page 27)	3/4 cup pecans (chopped)

1. When cheesecake is ready to be served, cut with a knife dipped in hot water. Top each slice with 1 tablespoon of caramel sauce and 1 tablespoon of pecans.

No-Bake Cheesecake
9 servings

Crust:

2 cups sugar-free cookie crumbs	1/4 cup butter (melted)

1. Combine cookie crumbs and butter in a small bowl. Toss to coat. Empty into an 8x8 baking dish. Press down with a fork to form crust.

Filling:

1 envelope unflavored gelatine	1/2 cup light agave
2/3 cup boiling water	1 teaspoon vanilla
2-8ounce packages cream cheese (softened)	

1. In a small bowl, combine boiling water and gelatine. Stir gelatine to completely dissolve. Set aside.
2. In a medium bowl, beat cream cheese, agave, and vanilla until smooth. Gradually beat in gelatine mixture. Pour over crust.
3. Refrigerate until set (approx. 3 hours). Cut into squares. Top with Berry Sauce (page 25).

Plain Cheesecake

12 servings

Crust:

1 cup whole wheat cracker crumbs	3 tablespoons light agave
1/2 cup pecans or walnuts (finely ground)	1 teaspoon ground cinnamon
6 tablespoons butter (melted)	

1. Preheat oven to 300°. Lightly butter sides of a 9-inch spring-form pan. Line bottom with parchment paper. Set aside.
2. In a small bowl combine cracker crumbs and nuts. Set aside.
3. In a separate bowl combine butter, agave, and cinnamon. Pour over cracker mixture. Stir to coat. Press into bottom of spring-form pan.
4. Prepare filling.

Filling:

3-8 ounce packages cream cheese (softened)	1 tablespoon lemon juice
3/4 cup light agave	1 teaspoon vanilla extract
3 eggs	

1. Place cream cheese in a large mixing bowl. With an electric mixer, gradually beat agave into cream cheese.
2. Beat in eggs, one at a time until smooth.
3. Stir in lemon juice and vanilla.
4. Pour over crust. Bake for 45 minutes or until center of cheesecake is firm.
5. Remove from oven. Turn oven off. Loosen sides of cheesecake with a knife. Place cheesecake back in oven. Leave in oven until pan is warm to the touch.
6. Cover and chill.
7. To make cutting easier, dip knife in hot water.
8. Serve plain or with sauce (see section "Sauces, Dressings, Toppings").

Thin-Mint Chocolate Torte

14 servings   Oven 350°

Crust:

6 tablespoons butter (softened)	3/4 cup whole wheat flour
1/3 cup light agave	1/3 cup cocoa powder

1. Preheat oven to 350°. Line a 9 1/2" spring-form pan with parchment paper. Set aside.
2. In a small bowl beat butter and agave.
3. Add flour and cocoa to form a thick batter.
4. With a rubber spatula spread batter in bottom of spring-form pan.
5. Bake for 8 minutes. Cool on wire rack while preparing filling.

Filling:

6 ounces unsweetened baking chocolate	2 tablespoons heavy cream
3/4 cup light agave	1 teaspoon peppermint extract
1 envelope unflavored gelatine	

1. In a small saucepan melt chocolate over medium heat.
2. Stir in agave. Bring to a boil. Remove from heat.
3. In a small bowl combine gelatine and 1/4 cup chocolate mixture. Stir thoroughly to dissolve gelatine. Return gelatine mixture to saucepan. Boil for 1 minute stirring continuously. Remove from heat.
4. Stir in heavy cream and peppermint extract.
5. Pour over crust. Cover and chill 2 hours before cutting.

Apple Pie

8 servings

Pastry for double pie crust (page 91)

5 cups green apples (peeled and thinly sliced)

2 teaspoons lemon juice

3/4 cup light agave

2 tablespoons butter

1/4 teaspoon salt

1/2 cup water

3 tablespoons cornstarch

1 1/2 teaspoons apple pie spice

1. Preheat oven to 400°.
2. In a medium saucepan combine apples and lemon juice. Toss to coat. Add agave, salt, and butter. Bring to a boil over medium-high heat. Boil until apples are tender.
3. In a small bowl combine water and cornstarch. Stir to dissolve. Add to apple mixture. Stir until mixture thickens. Remove from heat. Stir in apple pie spice.
4. Pour into 9" unbaked pie shell. Top with second pie crust. Seal edges. Pierce top with fork.
5. Bake 15-20 minutes or until crust is golden brown.

Blueberry Pie

8 servings

Pastry for double pie crust (page 91)	1/2 cup water
4 1/2 cups frozen blueberries	1/4 cup cornstarch
1 cup light agave	1 tablespoon lemon juice

1. Preheat oven to 375°.
2. In a medium saucepan combine frozen blueberries and agave.
3. In a small bowl combine water, cornstarch, and lemon juice. Add to saucepan. Stir.
4. Bring mixture to a boil over medium heat. Continue to stir until mixture thickens. Pour into a 9 1/2" pastry-lined pie plate. Add top crust. Seal edges.
5. Bake for 20-25 minutes or until crust is golden brown.

Chocolate Walnut Pie

8 servings

1 9-inch unbaked pie shell	2 tablespoons cocoa powder
3 eggs (beaten)	1/4 teaspoon salt
1/3 cup heavy cream	1 1/2 cups walnuts (chopped)
1 cup light agave	1/4 cup rolled oats
2 tablespoons butter (melted)	

1. Preheat oven to 350°.
2. In a medium bowl combine eggs, cream, agave, butter, cocoa powder, and salt. Whisk together until cocoa powder has dissolved. Stir in walnuts and oats.
3. Pour into a 9" pastry-lined pie plate.
4. Bake for 45 minutes.
5. Cool on wire rack. Filling flattens out as it cools. Serve at room temperature.

Coconut Cream Pie
8 servings

1 9-1/2" pie shell (pre-baked)	4 tablespoons cornstarch
1 cup unsweetened coconut flakes (toasted)	1 egg
	2 egg yolks
1 14-ounce can unsweetened coconut milk	2 tablespoons butter
1 envelope unflavored gelatine	1 teaspoon vanilla extract
1 cup light agave	

1. Pre-bake pie shell according to recipe directions. Set aside.
2. Preheat oven to 400° to toast coconut. Place coconut on rimmed baking sheet. Place in oven. Stir to toast evenly. Remove from oven when coconut is golden brown. Set aside.
3. In a small bowl combine unflavored gelatine and 1/2 cup coconut milk. Set aside.
4. In a medium saucepan, whisk remaining coconut milk, cornstarch, egg, egg yolks, and agave. Whisk continuously over medium heat until mixture thickens. Remove from heat. Whisk in gelatine mixture. Stir in butter, vanilla, and toasted coconut.
5. Transfer filling to a bowl. Cover surface of filling with plastic wrap. Chill 45 minutes. While chilling prepare topping (see next page).

Coconut Cream Pie (Cont.)

Topping:

2 cups heavy whipping cream	2 1/2 teaspoons coconut extract
4 tablespoons light agave	1/2 teaspoon cream of tartar

1. Beat cream, agave, coconut extract and cream of tartar with an electric mixer on high until stiff peaks form.
2. Remove filling from refrigerator. Fold half of whipped cream into filling. Pour into pre-baked pie shell. Cover with plastic wrap. Chill.
3. Refrigerate remaining whipped cream.
4. Top pie with remaining whipped cream when ready to serve.

Lemon Meringue Pie

8 servings

1 9-inch pie shell (pre-baked)	1/2 cup fresh lemon juice
6 tablespoons cornstarch	4 eggs (separated)
3 tablespoons unbleached white flour	1 cup light agave
1/4 teaspoon salt	2 tablespoons butter
1 cup water	Meringue (page 34)

1. Preheat oven to 350°.
2. In a medium saucepan combine cornstarch, flour, and salt. Whisk in water and lemon juice. Whisk in egg yolks and agave.
3. Cook over medium heat, stirring continuously. Cook until filling thickens. Remove from heat.
4. Add butter and stir until melted and thoroughly combined with custard.
5. Pour into baked pie shell. Set aside.
6. Prepare Meringue (page 34).
7. Pour meringue over filling, spreading it to the edge of pie crust.
8. Bake for 8-10 minutes or until meringue is golden.
9. Cool on wire rack. Cover and chill.

Peanut Butter Pie

12 servings

Crust:

2 cups cocktail peanuts (coarsely ground)	1/2 cup butter (melted)
1/2 cup whole wheat flour	1/4 cup light agave

1. Place peanuts in a blender. Blend on medium until peanuts are coarsely ground.
2. In a medium bowl combine peanuts, flour, butter, and agave. Mix thoroughly.
3. Pour mixture into a 9 or 9 1/2" pie pan. With a spoon spread peanut mixture in bottom of pan. Spread some of peanut mixture along sides of pan to form a crust.
4. Refrigerate crust while making filling.

Filling:

1-8 ounce package cream cheese (softened)	1 1/2 teaspoons vanilla extract
1 cup unsweetened creamy peanut butter	1 cup heavy cream
1 cup light agave	1/2 cup Chocolate Syrup (page 23)
2 tablespoons butter (softened)	

1. In a medium bowl, beat cream cheese, peanut butter, agave, butter, and vanilla together with an electric mixer until smooth. Set aside.
2. In a chilled metal bowl, beat heavy cream with an electric mixer until thick.
3. Fold whipped cream into peanut butter mixture. Mix.
4. Remove pie crust from refrigerator. Pour 1/4 cup of chocolate syrup onto bottom of pie crust. Pour filling on top of syrup. Pour evenly to prevent syrup from being pushed over sides of pie plate.
5. Cover and place in freezer for a few hours or overnight.
6. Before serving, garnish with remaining 1/4 cup of chocolate syrup.

Pecan Pie

8 servings

1 9-inch unbaked pie shell	4 tablespoons butter (melted)
3 eggs (beaten)	2 teaspoons vanilla extract
1/3 cup heavy cream	2 cups pecans (chopped)
1 cup light agave	1/4 teaspoon salt

1. Preheat oven to 325°.
2. In a medium bowl combine eggs, cream, agave, butter, and vanilla. Stir in pecans.
3. Pour into a 9-inch pastry-lined pie plate.
4. Bake for 55 minutes.
5. Cool on wire rack. Filling flattens out as it cools. Serve at room temperature.

Pumpkin Pie

8 servings

Oven 375°

Pastry for single pie crust (page 90)	1 1/2 teaspoons ground cinnamon
2 cups pumpkin (fresh or canned)	3/4 teaspoon ground ginger
1/2 cup heavy cream	3/4 teaspoon ground nutmeg
1/2 cup evaporated milk	1/4 teaspoon ground cloves
4 eggs (beaten)	3/4 teaspoon salt
3/4 cup light agave	2 teaspoons vanilla extract

1. Preheat oven to 375°.
2. In a large mixing combine all ingredients. Stir thoroughly.
3. Pour into 9 1/2" pastry-lined pie plate.
4. Bake for 45 minutes. Pie will be firm in middle when done.
5. Cool on wire rack. Cover and chill.

Whole Wheat and Oat Pie Crust

Yields one 9 1/2-inch crust   Oven 425°

1 1/4 cup whole wheat flour	1/2 cup butter (chilled)
1/2 cup oat flour	4 tablespoons cold water
1/2 teaspoon salt	

1. For pre-baked pie crust, preheat oven to 425°.
2. In a medium bowl stir together flours and salt.
3. Cut butter into flour until butter is pea-sized.
4. Form a well in the middle of flour. Add water one tablespoon at a time, using a fork to stir.
5. Form dough into a ball.
6. Place ball of dough between two pieces of parchment paper. Starting from center of dough roll out to edge until dough is 13 inches in diameter. Remove top piece of paper and carefully peel crust off of bottom paper.
7. Place crust in 9 1/2" pie pan. Trim excess crust off.
8. For pre-baked pastry shell, prick bottom and sides of pastry liberally before baking for 10 to 12 minutes or until golden.

Double Pie Crust

2 cups unbleached white flour	3/4 cup butter (chilled)
1/4 teaspoon salt	7-8 tablespoons ice water

1. In a medium bowl combine flour and salt.
2. Cut butter into flour until pieces of butter are pea-sized.
3. Make a well in middle of flour mixture.
4. Add water and toss with a fork to blend.
5. With hands form dough ball. Divide dough in half.
6. Place ball of dough between two pieces of parchment paper. Starting from center of dough roll out to edge until dough is 13 inches in diameter. Remove top piece of paper and carefully peel crust off of bottom paper.
7. Place crust in 9" or 9 1/2" pie pan (according to size specified in pie recipe). Trim excess crust off.
8. Add filling.
9. Repeat step 6 for second ball of dough. Lay top crust over filling. Pinch edges to seal. Pierce with fork or sharp knife in several places.
10. Bake according to selected recipe.

Ginger Spice Cookies

Yields 3 dozen

2 cups whole wheat flour	1 teaspoon ground ginger
2 teaspoons baking soda	3/4 cup butter (softened)
2 teaspoons ground cinnamon	1 cup dark agave
1 teaspoon ground cloves	2 eggs

1. Preheat oven to 325°.
2. In a medium bowl combine flour, baking soda, ground cinnamon, cloves, and ginger. Set aside.
3. In medium bowl beat agave into butter using electric mixer. Beat in eggs. Add to flour mixture. Stir. Cookie dough will be creamy in texture.
4. Drop by rounded tablespoon onto ungreased cookie sheet.
5. Bake 8-10 minutes. Cookies will be a dark golden brown.
6. Remove cookies from cookies sheet and place on paper towel-lined plate to cool completely.

Oatmeal Raisin Cookies

Yields 24 cookies

2 cups whole wheat flour	1/4 teaspoon ground cloves
2 cups rolled oats	1 cup light agave
1 teaspoon baking powder	3/4 cup butter (softened)
1/2 teaspoon baking soda	1 teaspoon vanilla extract
1/2 teaspoon cream of tartar	1 egg (beaten)
1 teaspoon ground cinnamon	

1. Preheat oven to 350°.
2. In a large bowl, combine flour, oats, baking powder, baking soda, cream of tartar, cinnamon, and cloves. Set aside.
3. In a medium saucepan add agave and butter. Bring to a boil over medium-high heat. Boil for 8 minutes. Remove from heat. Stir in vanilla. Pour over flour/oat mixture. Add raisins and egg. Stir to combine.
4. Drop by rounded tablespoons 3 inches apart on an ungreased cookie sheet.
5. Bake for 8 minutes. Press cookies flat with spatula for chewier results. Remove cookies from cookie sheet and place on a paper towel-lined plate to cool completely.

Peanut Butter Cookies

Yields 16 cookies

1 1/4 cup whole wheat flour	1/2 cup butter (softened)
1/4 cup peanuts (chopped)	1/2 cup unsweetened peanut butter
1/2 teaspoon baking powder	1 teaspoon vanilla extract
1/2 teaspoon baking soda	1 egg
3/4 cup light agave	

1. Preheat oven to 350°.
2. In a medium bowl combine flour, baking powder, baking soda, and peanuts. Set aside.
3. In a medium saucepan combine agave and butter. Bring to a boil over medium high heat. Boil for 8 minutes stirring frequently. Remove from heat. Stir in peanut butter and vanilla. Pour over flour mixture. Add egg. Stir to combine.
4. Take 1 heaping tablespoon of dough and roll into a ball. Place 3 inches apart on an ungreased cookie sheet. Flatten cookies using tines of fork. Bake for 7 to 9 minutes.
5. Remove cookies from cookie sheet and place on a paper towel lined-plate to cool completely.

Shortbread Cookies

Yields 20 cookies

3 cups unbleached white flour	1 cup butter (cut into small pieces)
1/4 cup arrowroot powder	2/3 cup light agave
1 teaspoon cream of tartar	

1. Preheat oven to 325°.
2. In a medium bowl combine flour, arrowroot powder, and cream of tartar. Cut butter into flour until butter is pea-sized.
3. Stir in agave until dough forms. Using hands, form dough into a ball. Roll dough out 1/2" thick on a lightly floured surface. Cut into 2-inch circles with a cookie or biscuit cutter. Place on ungreased cookie sheet.
4. Bake for 15 minutes. Remove cookies from cookie sheet and place on paper towel-lined plate to cool completely.

No-Bake Cookies

Yields 30 cookies

1 cup evaporated milk	1 cup unsweetened creamy peanut butter
2 cups light agave	1 teaspoon vanilla extract
1/2 cup butter	6 cups quick oats
1/2 cup cocoa powder	

1. In a medium saucepan add milk, agave, butter and cocoa powder.
2. Bring to a boil over medium heat. Boil for 5 minutes, stirring frequently. Remove from heat.
3. Stir in peanut butter and vanilla. Stir until peanut butter is mostly dissolved. Some of peanut butter may still be visible.
4. Place oatmeal into a large mixing bowl. Pour peanut butter mixture over oatmeal. Stir to coat.
5. Grease a 9x13 baking dish.
6. Pour cookie mixture into baking dish. Press down with spoon.
7. Refrigerate until firm. Cut into squares.

Peanut Butter Pie (page 87)

Cookie Bars

Yields 20 squares

Cookie Crust:

1 3/4 cup unbleached white flour	1/3 cup light agave
3 tablespoons arrowroot powder	3/4 cup unsweetened carob chips
1 teaspoon cream of tartar	3/4 cup pecans (chopped)
1/2 cup butter (cut into small pieces)	

1. Preheat oven to 350°. Grease 11x8x2 glass baking dish.
2. In a medium bowl combine flour, arrowroot powder, and cream of tartar. Cut butter into flour mixture until butter is pea-sized. Add agave and stir with spoon, working agave in until dough forms. Add carob chips and pecans. Stir to combine. Use hands to form dough ball.
3. Press dough firmly into prepared baking dish.
4. Bake 10 minutes. (While crust is baking prepare topping.)

Topping:

1 cup light agave	3/4 cup pecans (chopped)
3 tablespoon butter	1/2 cup unsweetened coconut flakes
1 teaspoon vanilla extract	
3/4 cup unsweetened carob chips	

1. In a small saucepan combine agave and butter. Bring to a boil over medium heat. Boil for 5 minutes, stirring occasionally. Remove from heat. Stir in vanilla. Pour mixture over crust. Set aside.
2. In a small bowl combine carob chips, pecans, and coconut flakes. Sprinkle evenly over top of agave mixture and press down with a fork.
3. Bake 20 minutes at 350°.
4. Place baking dish on wire rack to cool completely before cutting into squares.

Crispy Rice Peanut Squares

Yields 18 squares

1 cup light agave	1/2 cup dry roasted peanuts (coarsely chopped)
2 tablespoons butter	1/2 teaspoon vanilla extract
1/4 cup unsweetened creamy peanut butter	3 cups Brown Rice Crisps ™ (fruit juice sweetened, available in health food stores)
4 ounces cream cheese (softened)	

1. Preheat oven to 300°. Lightly grease an 8x11 glass baking dish.
2. Combine agave and butter in a small saucepan. Bring to a boil over medium heat. Boil for 10 minutes. Stir frequently. Remove from heat. Set aside.
3. In a large mixing bowl, beat cream cheese, peanut butter, and vanilla with an electric mixer until smooth. Stir in peanuts.
4. Add warm agave mixture and crispy brown rice cereal.
5. Stir until cereal is thoroughly coated.
6. Pour cereal mixture into prepared baking dish. Spread evenly with a spoon.
7. Bake for 15 minutes. Remove from oven. Allow to cool in dish. Cut into squares. Transfer to a covered container. Store in refrigerator.

Chewy Granola Bars

18 servings

2 cups oatmeal	1 cups almonds (chopped)
2 cups crispy brown rice cereal	1 1/2 cup light agave
1 cup puffed millet	2 tablespoons butter
1/2 cup toasted wheat germ	2 teaspoons vanilla extract
1 cup dried fruit pieces	
1 cup dry roasted peanuts (finely ground)	

1. In a large mixing bowl combine dry ingredients. Set aside.
2. In a medium saucepan bring agave to a boil over medium heat. Remove from heat. Stir in butter and vanilla. Pour over dry ingredients. Stir to coat.
3. Lightly grease a 9x13 baking dish.
4. Pour mixture into dish. Spread and press down firmly with a spoon. Using spoon or palm of hand to pack mixture tightly.
5. Allow to completely cool before cutting.

Fudge Brownie Pudding

6 servings

Batter:

3/4 cup whole wheat flour	1/4 cup butter (melted)
1/4 cup cocoa powder	1/4 cup light agave
1 1/2 teaspoon baking powder	2 teaspoons vanilla extract
1/2 teaspoon salt	1/4 cup hot water
1/4 cup sour cream	2 tablespoons instant coffee

1. Preheat oven to 275°. Grease a 2-quart casserole dish.
2. In a medium bowl, combine flour, cocoa, baking powder, and salt. Set aside.
3. In a medium bowl, whisk together sour cream, butter, agave, and vanilla. In a small bowl, combine water and instant coffee. Stir to dissolve. Add to sour cream mixture. Whisk.
4. Add sour cream mixture to dry ingredients. Stir until thick batter forms. Spread evenly in bottom of prepared dish. Set aside.
5. Prepare topping.

Topping:

1 cup water	2 tablespoons instant coffee
2/3 cup light agave	1 teaspoon vanilla extract
1/4 cup cocoa powder	

1. In a small saucepan, combine water, agave, and cocoa. Bring to a boil over medium heat. Boil five minutes, stirring occasionally.
2. Remove from heat. Stir in instant coffee and vanilla extract.
3. Pour topping mixture over batter. Cover.
4. Bake for 25 minutes. When done, the topping will have formed pudding at the bottom of the brownie. Top with whipped cream (page 35) and chopped pecans if desired.

Caramel Popcorn with Almonds

Yields 8 cups

1 gallon air-popped popcorn	1 teaspoon vanilla extract
1/2 cup butter	1/4 teaspoon baking soda
1 cup light agave	1 cup whole almonds

1. Preheat oven to 250°.
2. In a small saucepan, melt butter. Add agave and bring to a boil over medium heat. Boil for 5 minutes. Stir frequently. Remove from heat. Stir in vanilla and baking soda.
3. Place popped corn in a roasting pan. Pour mixture over popped corn. Stir to coat. Add almonds and stir.
4. Bake for one hour. Stir every 15 minutes.
5. Remove from oven and cool.
6. As mixture cools, stir occasionally to break up any large clumps that form. Transfer to an airtight container.

Butterscotch Pudding

8 servings

1/2 cup water	1/4 cup dark agave
3 tablespoons cornstarch	2 12-ounce cans evaporated milk
6 tablespoons butter	3 eggs yolks (beaten)
3/4 cup light agave	1 teaspoon vanilla

1. In a small bowl combine water and cornstarch. Set aside.
2. In a medium saucepan bring butter and agave to a boil over medium heat. Boil for 5 minutes, stirring continuously. Add evaporated milk and cornstarch water. Return to a boil. Remove from heat.
3. Take 1 cup of hot mixture and slowly stir into beaten eggs. Return egg mixture to saucepan. Stir over medium heat until mixture boils and thickens. Remove from heat. Stir in vanilla.
4. Transfer to a bowl and cover surface of pudding with plastic wrap. Chill.

Chocolate Pudding

8 servings

4 ounces unsweetened baking chocolate (melted)	1/4 cup cornstarch
	1/2 teaspoon salt
2 2/3 cups milk	1/4 cup butter
1 cup light agave	2 teaspoons vanilla extract
4 egg yolks (beaten)	

1. In a medium saucepan whisk together melted chocolate, milk, agave, egg yolks, cornstarch, and salt.
2. Bring to a boil over medium heat, whisking frequently. When mixture boils and thickens, remove from heat.
3. Stir in butter and vanilla. Butter should be completely melted.
4. Transfer to a bowl and cover surface of pudding with plastic wrap. Chill.

Vanilla Pudding

8 servings

2 2/3 cups milk	1/2 teaspoon salt
3/4 cup light agave	1/4 cup butter
2 eggs (beaten)	1 tablespoon vanilla extract
1/4 cup cornstarch	

1. In a medium saucepan whisk together milk, agave, eggs, cornstarch, and salt. Bring to a boil over medium heat, whisking frequently. When mixture boils and thickens, remove from heat.
2. Stir in butter and vanilla. Butter should be completely melted.
3. Transfer to a bowl and cover surface of pudding with plastic wrap. Chill.

Chocolate Ice Cream
Yields 1 quart

3 1/2 cups half and half	1 teaspoon vanilla extract
1 cup light agave	1 teaspoon almond extract
3 egg yolks	3 ounces unsweetened baking chocolate (melted)
1 envelope unflavored gelatine	

1. In a medium saucepan whisk together half and half, agave, egg yolks, and unflavored gelatine. Bring to a boil over medium heat while constantly whisking. Remove from heat. Strain mixture to remove any egg that may have formed during cooking process.
2. Stir in melted chocolate, vanilla, and almond extracts.
3. Transfer to a container. Cover and chill.
4. Chill completely before freezing according to ice cream maker's directions.

Vanilla Ice Cream

Yields 2 cups

3 1/2 cups half and half	4 egg yolks
2/3 cup light agave	2 teaspoons vanilla extract

1. In a medium saucepan whisk together half and half, agave, and egg yolks. Bring to a boil over medium heat while constantly whisking. Remove from heat. Strain mixture to remove any egg that may have formed during cooking process. Stir in vanilla.
2. Cover and chill.
3. Chill completely before freezing according to ice cream maker's directions.

Pumpkin Ice Cream

Yields 1 quart

2 cups whole milk	1/4 teaspoon ground cloves
2/3 cup light agave	1 teaspoon vanilla extract
5 egg yolks	1 cup pumpkin pie filling (unsweetened)
1 teaspoon salt	
1 teaspoon ground cinnamon	1 pre-baked pie crust (broken into small pieces)
1/4 teaspoon ground ginger	Caramel Sauce (page 27)
1/4 teaspoon ground nutmeg	

1. In a medium saucepan, whisk together milk, agave, egg yolks, salt, and spices. Bring to a boil over medium heat while constantly whisking. Remove from heat after mixture thickens slightly. Strain mixture to remove any egg that may have formed during cooking process. Whisk in pumpkin and vanilla.
2. Transfer to a container. Cover and chill.
3. Chill completely before freezing according to ice cream maker's directions.
4. Top each serving of ice cream with Caramel Sauce and pieces of pie crust.

Raspberry Sorbet

Yields 3 cups

5 cups raspberries (other berries may be substituted) 3/4 cup light agave	1/3 cup water 2 tablespoons lemon juice

1. Place all ingredients in a blender (or food processor). Blend until smooth.
2. Pour mixture through a fine mesh strainer using a rubber spatula to press through.
3. Cover and chill.
4. Chill completely before freezing according to ice cream maker's directions.

For Kids

Caramel Dip with Apples

5 servings

Caramel Sauce (page 27)	5 medium apples (quartered with seeds removed)

1.   Serve cut apples with 1/4 cup Caramel Sauce per apple.

Fresh Fruit Popsicles

Servings vary

1 cup boiling water	2 cups fresh fruit
1 envelope unflavored gelatine	2/3 cup light agave

1. In a small bowl combine boiling water and gelatine. Stir to completely dissolve.
2. Place gelatine mixture, fruit, and agave in a blender. Blend until fruit is desired consistency. Pour into popsicle molds. Leave room at the top for expansion as it freezes. Add popsicle sticks.
3. Freeze at least 6 hours.

Frozen Cream Delight

Yields 4 cups

2 cups fat-free milk or unsweetened soy milk	1 envelope unsweetened drink mix
3/4 cup light agave	1 cup heavy cream

1. In a freezer-safe container combine agave, milk, and drink mix. Mix until drink mix dissolves. Place in freezer for several hours until mixture is slushy.
2. In a small bowl beat cream with an electric mixer until stiff. Fold whipped cream into milk mixture until thoroughly combined.
3. Place in freezer for 2 more hours. Use ice cream scoop to serve.

Fudgesicles
Servings vary

12 ounces silken tofu	3/4 cup light agave
4 ounces unsweetened baking chocolate	1/2 teaspoon salt
1/4 cup heavy cream	1 teaspoon vanilla
	3 egg whites

1. Remove tofu from package and pat with several paper towels to absorb moisture. Set aside.
2. In a medium pan combine baking chocolate, cream, agave, and salt. Bring to a boil over medium heat. Stir frequently. Remove from heat.
3. In a blender combine drained tofu, vanilla and egg whites. Pour chocolate mixture in blender. Blend on high until all tofu is completely blended.
4. When filling popsicle forms leave room at the top for expansion as it freezes. Insert popsicle sticks and place in freezer.
5. Freeze for at least 8 hours.

Ice Cream in a Bag

1 serving

1/2 cup half and half	6 cups of ice
1 tablespoon light agave	1 zipper seal sandwich bag
1/4 teaspoon vanilla	1-quart zipper seal plastic bag
6 tablespoons rock salt	

1. In sandwich bag combine half and half, agave, and vanilla. Seal tightly.
2. In 1-quart plastic bag add 2 cups of ice. Sprinkle 2 tablespoons rock salt over ice. Place sealed sandwich bag on top of ice. Continue to layer 2 cups of ice sprinkled with 2 tablespoons of rock salt until bag is filled with ice.
3. Seal bag. Wrap kitchen towel around bag. Shake bag vigorously back and forth for 10 minutes. Ensure sandwich bag stays surrounded by ice. After 10 minutes, mixture should resemble soft-serve ice cream.
4. Place bag in freezer for 15 minutes to harden.
5. Remove bag from freezer. Remove sandwich bag from ice. Eat straight from sandwich bag or scrape ice cream into a cup.

Brown Rice Crispy Treats

9 servings

3 cups Brown Rice Crisps ™ (fruit juice sweetened, available in health food stores) 1/2 cup light agave	2 tablespoons butter 1 teaspoon vanilla extract

1. In a medium saucepan combine agave and butter. Bring to a boil over medium heat. Boil for 5 minutes. Remove from heat. Stir in vanilla. Add brown rice cereal. Stir to coat.
2. Line an 8x8 baking dish with parchment paper. Spread mixture with a spoon.
3. Cool before cutting into squares.

Soft Raisin Granola Bars

15 servings   Oven 325°

3 cups rolled oats	1 cup light agave
1 1/2 cups whole wheat flour	1 cup plain yogurt
2 teaspoons ground cinnamon	1/4 cup vegetable oil
1 teaspoon baking soda	2 teaspoons vanilla extract
1/2 teaspoon salt	1 cup raisins
2 eggs, beaten	

1.   Preheat oven to 325°. Grease a 9x13 baking dish. Set aside.
2.   In a large bowl combine oats, flour, cinnamon, baking soda, and salt. Set aside.
3.   In a small bowl combine eggs, agave, yogurt, oil, and vanilla. Add to dry ingredients. Stir. Fold in raisins.
4.   Spread dough evenly in prepared dish.
5.   Bake 35 minutes or until slightly brown.
6.   Cool on wire rack. Cut into rectangles.

Pumpkin Sandwich Cookies

Yields 25

3 1/2 cups whole wheat flour	1 15-ounce can pumpkin (unsweetened)
2 teaspoons ground cinnamon	
1 teaspoon ground ginger	1 1/2 cups light agave
1/2 teaspoon ground cloves	3/4 cup vegetable oil
1 teaspoon baking powder	3 eggs
1 teaspoon baking soda	1 teaspoon vanilla extract
1 teaspoon salt	Cream Cheese Frosting (page 72)

1. Preheat oven to 350°
2. In a medium bowl combine dry ingredients. Set aside.
3. In a large bowl beat together pumpkin, agave, oil, eggs, and vanilla extract. Slowly mix in dry ingredients.
4. Drop by rounded tablespoon onto an ungreased cookie sheet.
5. Bake 8-10 minutes or until firm.
6. Place cookies on rack to cool. While cookies are cooling prepare Cream Cheese Frosting.
7. After cookies have completely cooled, frost flat side of 1st cookie and place second cookie on top, flat side facing frosting to form sandwich. Store in refrigerator.

Gelatine Squares
Yields 20 squares

1 cup light agave	2 cups + 1/2 cup water
1 envelope unsweetened drink mix	3 envelope unflavored gelatine

1. Combine unsweetened drink mix, 2 cups water, and agave in a small saucepan. Bring to a boil. Remove from heat.
2. In a medium bowl combine 1/2 cup water and gelatine. Allow to set for 1 minute then add hot agave mixture. Stir until gelatine dissolves.
3. Pour into an 8x11 pan. Place in refrigerator until firm. Cut into squares.

Popcorn Balls

Yields 14 balls

---

13 cups popped popcorn (unpopped kernels removed)

1 cup light agave

1 tablespoon butter

1/2 teaspoon salt

1/2 teaspoon vanilla extract

---

1. Preheat oven to 275°.
2. Place popped popcorn in large roasting pan. Place in oven to keep warm.
3. In a small saucepan bring agave, butter, and salt, to a boil over medium heat. Boil for 8 minutes. Agave should reach hard ball stage before removing from heat. Test temperature with candy thermometer.
4. Remove from heat. Stir in vanilla.
5. Remove popcorn from oven. Pour agave mixture evenly over popcorn. Stir to coat.
6. Allow mixture to cool slightly before forming into balls.
7. To form balls, lightly oil hands. Take approximately 1 cup of popcorn in hands and form a ball. Press ball firmly together. Place on wax paper.

Root Beer

4 servings

1 1-liter bottle club soda (chilled)   1 tablespoon root beer extract

1/3 cup light agave

1.   Combine all ingredients in a large pitcher. Stir thoroughly.
     Pour over ice. Serve immediately.

Cream of Tomato Soup

Yields 8 cups

3 tablespoons butter	1 6-ounce can tomato paste
1/3 cup whole wheat flour	1 46-ounce can tomato juice
1 cup milk or unsweetened soy milk	1/3 cup light agave

1. In a large saucepan melt butter over medium heat. Slowly stir in flour to make a thick paste. Gradually add milk, stirring constantly to blend. Add tomato paste, tomato juice, and agave.
2. Continue to stir over medium heat until all ingredients are blended and soup is hot.

Index